Carnal Fragrance

Also by Florence Weinberger

The Invisible Telling Its Shape

Breathing Like A Jew

Carnal Fragrance

poems

FLORENCE WEINBERGER

Red Hen Press ⬥ Los Angeles

Carnal Fragrance

Cover art *Venus, Ariadne and Bacchus* by Jerald Silva

Book design by Michael Vukadinovich
Cover Design by Mark E. Cull

ISBN 1-888996-95-1

Library of Congress Catalog Card Number 2004096618

Published by Red Hen Press

The City of Los Angeles Cultural Affairs Department, California Arts Council and the Los Angeles County Arts Commission partially support Red Hen Press.

First Edition

Acknowledgments

This is my Academy Award Acceptance Speech, my first opportunity to thank the fabulous people who have been part of my poetry life for over 40 years, critics/friends, workshop teachers, beloved poets who have died, living poets I have loved:

Elaine Alarcon, Trudy Alexy, Richard Beban, Kate Braverman, Judy Brayer, Jean Brody, Christopher Buckley, Ralph S. Carlson, Nels Christianson, Jeanette Clough, Wanda Coleman, Carol V. Davis, Fred Franklyn, Helen Friedland, Kate Gale, Amy Gerstler, Shirley Graham, Jack Grapes, Steve Gross, Doris Grumbach, Robert Hass, Karen Holden, Ro Jaeger, Gloria Jagudin, Robin Johnson, Galway Kinnell, Carol Kivo, Carolyn Kizer, Norm Levine, Peggy Levine, Peter Levitt, Shirley Love, Glenna Luschei, Lee McCarthy, Anne Marple, Henry J. Morro, Lisel Mueller, Jim Natal, Linda Neal, Terri Niccum, Sharon Olds, David Oliveira, Sherman Pearl, Mima Pereira, Irwin Porges, Holly Prado, Ellen Reich, Harriet Rochlin, Sarah Rose Rolfe, Lee Rossi, David St. John, Benjamin Saltman, Nina Sandrich, Joyce Schwartz, Robin Schyman, Anne Silver, Lila Silvern, Doris Silverton, Maurya Simon, Carol Stager, Ann Stanford, Joyce Stein, Gerald Stern, Austin Straus, Phil Taggart, Carine Topal, Amy Uyematsu, Carol Walker, Jan Wesley, Jackson Wheeler, Bayla Winters, Cecilia Woloch, and Sondra Zeidenstein

Poems have appeared in the following periodicals, some in different form:

Artlife: "To Imagine"; *Beyond the Valley of the Contemporary Poets (1998):* "The Tailor's Widow Cooks for One," published as "My First Saturday Night Home Alone Is"; *Daybreak:* "I Could Say It's Tobacco"; *Rattle:* "I Began With Frayed Swaters," "Evicting the Mourning Doves"; *Rivertalk:* "How the Dead Crowd Our Closets," "The Night Draws Itself Around My Throat"; *The Cancer Poetry Project:* "Numb"; *Spillway:* "A New Owner," "She Put on Your Hat."

Contents

Carnal Fragrance

Walking on Ashes

We dared, we went just the same, our eyes enormous and blameless
in the bright mustard light of Rome. Wet beside the ashes of Pompeii,
under the shadow of Vesuvius, we stumbled through deep drifts of cinders.
We kept up, kept walking through their ruined kitchens, past their altars swept
clean of offerings, past the phalli still guarding the blasted doorways.
Through sun and rain we kept up, alongside
the bodies caught asleep or stunned or staring. Kept up
until we reached the healing shining waters off the Amalfi coast.
And so we were briefly undismayed,

grateful to absorb its excess, the bravely balanced houses, churches
yanked toward heaven by their blue-gold mosaic domes, ropes of garlic,
tomatoes, peppers
piled spicy red against the blue sea. We flexed our legs and kept up.
We climbed the streets and wide steps of Positano, always turning,
cognizant of the vast sea behind us, the distant continent,
the monumental size of these distractions.
On your thigh that small button the color of dirty blood grew bigger,
and we both knew we were going back to the rest—
malevolent seedlings boiling, already bursting, flowing
in rivulets under your skin.

It Began

It began with randomness, the fabulous
violent smell of first attraction. It veered
like a runaway bus into a reckless marriage, lust
to merge, to be wholly known, to be let alone.
We became parents.

Empty nesters.
Fierce wrestlers still holding hands in the movies.
Settled at last into an edgy accommodation,
we began growing old softened
by the balm of intimacy.

There must have been something left smoldering.

It began with a mole
that became a seedbed of hot dislocations,
the yes and no of what we would and would not do.

No one else saw it, just we two.
No seer or physician was consulted
while its power grew
to split us apart. One of us afraid, one furious.

One is afraid, one justifies.
One denies, one badgers. One postpones,
one shrugs. Both are afraid.

For a year the fear was folded and unfolded
and when at last the diagnosis came,
I nearly smiled to be so cruelly vindicated.

Waiting Out Your Surgery

Waiting. Waiting is pacing.
Waiting is kaleidoscopic, there
are prisms of anxiety, blinding facets
to my impatience,

broken glass under my feet
and what attention falls on.
Patients and magazines expire here.
My stomach hurts.

The umbilical phone
in the waiting room
ravels into the surgery.
When it rings, even the children
stop talking, and every head turns.

If I turn too fast,
I'll fall out of balance.
What does *hours* mean?
What destiny determines the stealth
of my breathing?
Am I imagining, or have I grown dull
from holding my breath?
What more could I have done
to get ready for this?

It takes the church years
to confirm
a single miracle.

In Love With the Doctor

We both fall in love with the blunt doctor.
We bless his hands that have cut out the malignancy.
We trace the tracks on your skin as if they are the history of medicine: this
is how far we have come since Hippocrates.
In a post-op haze we hear him chronicle deep excisions, dying nodes, the blind
persistence of mobile cells.
We are hung on his doomed predictions.
We transform the words as they drop from his mouth.
We look into his eyes for contradictions, for hope, for godliness.
We hope he is not tired.
We listen without crying out, as if we are intelligent and grateful.
We have the right to ask questions.
If we are intelligent enough, we will ask the right questions, so the doctor
can give us the right answers.

The Hospital

The hospital reeks so much of doom, of too much
chlorine, it's a screaming cliché of a place, gray
food and smutch-green walls, the clattering, saddening afternoons,
midnight wakenings to draw blood, force pills, check the pulse, the tubes,
the TV, the fevers, the blankets, the slope of the bed, the heat in the room,
the lay of the land.
A plastic bracelet's at your wrist with your name, you won't be mistaken
for someone else but nobody knows who you are.
There is only this to get through and the next day and enough days
until I notice you're alive enough to speak
the words you're almost too drugged to say distinctly: *Take me home.*

Home

Cut, scarred, bandaged, doubled over with pain, you are home.
You want to heal. You have been deprived of work.
You want to sleep without pain. You want to go to the bathroom without pain.
You simply want to sit up and reach for a book, you want to have desire back,
to speak to a friend, to go outdoors, to pick up the leaves,
to sit in your car, to have a destination.

I want you to sleep without pain. I want you to go to the bathroom
without pain. I want you simply to sit up and reach for a book.
I want you to have desire back, to reach for a spoon or a glass,
to take the phone from my hand and speak to a friend. I want you
outside picking up leaves that have fallen all over the yard.
I want you sitting in your car, turning the key, going somewhere.

Pain in the Morning

You said the pain is sweetest at dawn.
It is congealed from sleeping, pressed down hard
into the mattress as if practicing eternity in wet loam.
You have been lying in it all night long.
Light at morning assures
you are still in life, bearing it, leaving it behind,
and leaving it behind, even for a second, defeating it.

You say none of these things. They are not even my dream,
they are made-up lines, as if the pain is mine to play with.
I can smooth your face. I can take the chronic ache in my right hip
and move it around. A man I know said don't chase pain,
it will find a place in you if it wishes to stay.

Of this I am certain: I know every sound your body makes.

Epidemic

Friends were falling all around us.
I felt lucky, untouched, puzzled how it skipped around us.
My father, aunts, cousins, more friends,
as if we lived on a street in Bosnia
where every wall had bullet holes and every
doorstep except ours was stained with blood.
Then it was you.
What do I do?
I have not kept even the simplest word of each commandment.
I have not smeared my doorpost with sacrificial blood;
grace is mine.
My shame is no secret; I'm glad it's not me.
I protest that I'm human. For now I'm relieved.
But I won't tell you. But I won't tell you.

Scaling Ice

It is something like scaling ice.
Pausing at the faultlines
to breathe.
A treatment every four weeks.
The gift of increments building in the blood.
The twisted wreckage of the sweet word *treat*.
The room frigid. The wait long. We talk about later.
I hum, we read, you doze, until at last the nurse comes.
You are not a child;
she won't conceal what she holds in her hand. Deft
and swift, she sticks the needle under your skin, eight times,
raising welts like little hills while you lie on your back, your legs rigid,
your eyes pinched shut, squeezing my hand
as if it is a lifeline attached to solid rock. I force my mind
to be here. To keep my hold,
the soles of my feet must attach to the earth.
But I feel suspended.
Like hanging, this kind of isolation.
Around me the walls of present time are hard, high
and slippery. Stay here. Watch this. This is not the horizon,
this is not a mind-trail on an endless sky, a few drags on a joint
to the point of oblivion, the draining of a glass of wine, this is not
nostalgia for the fifties when we married,
this is not charity or literature.
This is a present
that nevertheless moves, it moves past this moment, it moves
to the next, it moves with the breath, it moves like a sentence,
by syllables, by intervals, it moves forward with the breath
until at last you loosen your grip on my hand and your legs come down
and your teeth unclench and you lie back.

To Imagine

To survive the Shoah and die in your bed,
you had to be brilliant with imagination.
You had to be invisible
while the life on the inside boiled with indignation
and desire.
You called it luck.
For years we argued while I tried to convince you
that God and prescience were your true garments.
All you would grant was the chance of our meeting.

You Dream About Eating An Egg

No one loved eggs the way you did.
Ate your way through dozens, soft-boiled and scrambled.

Taught your granddaughter how to spoon them
out of the shell.

Ate them pure without salt or butter or ham.
Without guilt.

Careful not to lose a drop.
That's why your dream about the yolk spilling out

when you bit into the hot golden center of the egg
scared me to death.

Photographs

I have only this to go by: What you told me of a boy barely out of his teens
returning home from the death camps; his parents, his siblings, his belongings gone,
his young history looted. All that remained were old mildewed photographs flung
to the farthest corners of your naked rooms like uprooted populations of Jews.

When you left forever you took them along; they'd remain what they were, coded
bits of lost lives you brought me like a dowry of golden coins. Hard-earned proofs,
they froze in place the missing bones of your family. Later, on a friend's dresser
in post-war Germany, you first saw my family, spiffed up, splendid as an artifact.

Every picture my father sent my cousin Jack from America contained the myth of
truth, a slight tint of distortion, a whiff of prosperity. For years you've told everyone
how you were smitten by a black and white photograph composed in a studio. I hated
the way the high cut of that dress made my breasts seem enormous. I was fifteen.

My sister sat next to me, my parents stood, flanking us like righteous pillars.
What did you see? Weren't the banked unsorted ashes still clouding your eyes?
How come you chose me? Couldn't you tell I was myopic, my smile coerced,
my hands idle in my lap? Couldn't you see I was unequipped? Husband:

What made you think that raw girl showed promise enough
to last you your life? We have since filled albums with travels, filtering out the sun,
the compromises. We didn't know then how it is possible to manipulate an image.
I wouldn't take your picture now, you've lost too much flesh.

I don't know how to trick the lens, to bring back again the body I feed and feed
praying your muscular frame returns. Cancer bends your bones, turns your eyes
inward toward the pain, revives an older pain, the pictures you saved loose
in a box you've carried over fifty years. Those pictures send the story back to me.

They ask me to define who I became, since you are in the dream of medication
and still in love. I haven't stopped to think for months, as if your body has become
a rough road that needs a desolated driver's vigilance. Think of this as one of a series:
Snapshots taken from a distant planet, me headed toward a destination I cannot see.

Getting In Bed With a Man Who Is Sick

Every night I get in bed with a man who is sick.
I have to move fluidly and stiffly,
as if a healthy thrust
under the blankets, a shift
of my body to find the right spot
could cause his body to end up in agony.
All through the night, in my sleep,
I hear his moans,
constant now as breathing.
His flesh is disappearing.
More and more I see his bones. In some places
I see right through his skin
to the blue-pebbled tumors
erupting there, pushing in two ways,
toward the light and toward the death
of their unwilling host.
His breathing is labored. His voice
has changed. Tonight
he kissed me back brief and hard with a strength
I thought I'd never know from him again.
See, it said, I remember. I wonder
if that will become one of those moments
we tend not to forget; that come to be
all of it together, so we can say it
sometime in the future
in one sentence
and don't have to replay the life and the dying over
and over again. When we are sleeping
alone, and we wake, and the walls are breathing,
and they are the company we keep.

The Watch

It's such a disrupted life,
you dying, me cooking more than you can possibly eat.

You're turning whiter, the light is beginning to show through your skin,
the glow cancer makes as it burns up the body from within.
When I'm close to you and your mouth opens to speak, I smell the combustion.

I don't know the pain no matter how simple your description.
Where do you stretch on the scale between now
and the end of your life? What is the function of endurance?

I imagine you in your place of business, alone, overtaken by fatigue.
Like a night guard in the citadel. Fighting to stay awake.
This time you fight off the ghosts who want you to live out the past with them.
You come home, lie down, sink quickly into a deep untroubled sleep.

Once I described you with metaphoric pockets full of seeds.
Once I described you as young, blushing.

I've described you remote, stubborn, addictive.
I always left the bite in. I didn't want to forget the bite
that would then let me sneak in the sweetness.

Sleep. This is my watch.

My Tenderness

My sister says she is moved that I am so tender with him.
Why shouldn't I be?
He didn't plan to die like this,

his arms thin as wire, nearly transparent,
his eyes deep in his face
the way he must have looked

fifty years ago, when he walked out of the death camps
and went home; he is still astonished
he lived through that long impossibility.

Now that he has learned to love life again
to lose it again. Why shouldn't I
touch him, my sorrow turned to muscle

while I lift him to his feet,
my voice ordinary, as if it is ordinary
to die accompanied by tenderness.

Easy

I whispered in your ear so softly,
I'm not sure I wanted you to hear me.

It's so easy, I said, over and over,
wanting the horror of my instruction

to sink below the sound of the words
so you would hear only the love,

so you would know suffering can end softly,
like shutting off a piece of machinery—

your old Singer sewing machine
before you closed your tailor shop,

the careful dusting, the covering up
the way we drape the dead.

But that wasn't easy for you,
laying down your work passion

like a retiring king taking off his crown,
or letting our long marriage unravel,

leaving our children
to tell their children the great point of the story.

When your breathing became shallow
I never stopped whispering

all through the night, my love, rumors of hope.
Later the others arrived and took up the watch.

You did not betray me. You said nothing to them
with your very last breath.

Evicting the Mourning Doves

They were clearly mated for life.
They hung around a few days,
enough time for me to speculate
which potted plant they'd choose for nesting.
If it turned out to be the cascading succulent, my favorite,
would I be afraid they'd stifle it
with their bits of string and trash.
Now that I had memorized their song and named them mourning doves,
would I rage, would I turn them out.
Would I coldly spill their nest on the ground.

Suddenly they were gone. I will have to mourn alone.
I will have to batter the air with my arms and kick the impacted soil
until it opens.
I will have to buy a coffin.
I will have to make arrangements.
I will not be able to imitate their song in my throat.
I will have to form words.
I will have to choose burial clothes.
I will have to forego flight and symmetry and the harboring of nests.
I will have to wait for spring in a different year, and without you.

Gasping

There was no precedent in my life for your death. My mother
was killed by an anaesthesiologist
or a surgeon concealed behind swinging doors. I wasn't there.
My father died sitting upright in front of the TV.
His sister died in whispers of the Big C when I was three.
A mass family destruction surmised when the ashes of Auschwitz were sifted.
But you lay dying for hours in full view of the children.
Nieces and nephews came and went
as if they were dipping into a novel.
A skillful nurse with a sense of the ways a man's body drifts away
piled pillows around you, and the ancestors waited.
You breathed your last breaths in a rasping ichorous rhythm
I had only read about in literature,
which I have fortunately forgotten
for how could I effectively render it?

Numb

It is hard to give up after months of making lists,
phoning doctors, fighting entropy. But when the end comes,
a bending takes over, empties the blood of opposition
and with a gentle skill, injects a blessed numbness.
I know the air around me thinned when he stopped breathing,
and though I did not faint, I could not stand
to stay and watch his dank soiled clothes removed, his body
turned and washed and shrouded.
Someone led me out and someone sat me down
and someone held me. I heard a sound leave my mouth,
unearthly, unfamiliar. I uttered it only once.
A few days later I dress carefully, as if the habit instilled in a woman
who dresses for public appearances is as much a scar
as a vaccination is. I let others take care of the particulars.
Perhaps this surrender foreshadows my own old age
when I have raged to exhaustion and finally have to go.
The numbness wears off. I drive to the market, cook my own food,
take scant note of desire
with no one else to consider or contradict my choices.
Something in me will never go on. Something in me will go on.

Prayer

Of course I prayed.
Partly out of habit; I prayed as a child without learning how,

without knowing what haunting necessity possessed me then.
So when it seemed certain

my husband, my partner of my entire adult life was going to die,
I prayed the hardest prayer: *Thy will be done.*

I was giving up arguments, bargaining, recriminations. The carnal
fragrance of hope.

Except for an almost inaudible request for mercy, I would go on living
with *Thy will.* Except for an almost unquenchable quest for meaning

I would go on laying down one word after another with trembling,
shaking, dwelling with moving lips on the relentless decay

and the way we love the children of our children; what it means
to leave an absence behind. What it is: to leave.

But would I be able to skirt the divinity and order and moral protest of poetry?
And how else to obliterate the glibness of death by cancer?

I began pounding these Kabbalistic questions on Afro-Cuban drums and found
I could reach pure anger by banging beyond concept.

Drumming with other women and men I became a lunatic drumming
my frenzy in chorus on bare nerve briefly giving up my quest for meaning.

Hearing how grief and heartbeat augmented each other
I began to regain my personal sense of desire.

I kept walking rapidly early in the morning, chanting
conviction under my breath

talking about him to everybody I came across
not caring that they seemed uncomfortable

baffled
that I let him die in the house in the bed on the side where I will never sleep

dosing him with almost invisible tabs of morphine
forced past his lips and under his tongue

to melt like hot snow the more swiftly to enter his blood stream
fully understanding intervals and ultimate objective

and why it is I can now bring myself to remember
as many details as I can bear

and I can keep walking and chanting and drumming *thy will*
and I can call it prayer and I can keep praying and praying

that someday my will comes closer to yours, O Lord.

When You Knew Yourself

Whose face did you see first?
No one in your family, I hope,
for how could they
tend you toward deliverance
when the last faces they saw
were the strangers'
who murdered them.
I suspect it was Ruth's.
She'd just gotten there herself
but she'd been practicing for years.
So I suspect she held her hand out to you
though you hadn't really been friends,
and you took it, because you knew
I trusted her. That's when you saw
the others, one at a time, all dead
and yet they existed not as distorted
memories but solid in a circle around you
shoulder to shoulder, each
familiar face now folding
into the next, until you were
recognized. Then you knew yourself,
and your journey began.

The Tailor's Widow Cooks For One

My first Saturday night home alone is
honed in whim and smoke. Flowers
of steamed broccoli added to my pasta
assure my guardian angel
that I watch out for myself too.
Sweet juicy watermelon, as much
balance as I could find in my
refrigerator. I cook conscious
and half-mad, for one mouth, for speed,
throwing in anise seed, a clove of garlic, inventing
a new dish, as befits a new widow who is
going to live a long and healthy life.
That wedged whiff of creativity
lets me know I have begun
to bend the minutes to myself.
I iron, too,
while operatic overtures billow like silk
through the empty rooms.
And I sew, as I saw him in his shop
listening to Beethoven, or sitting home beside me
sewing, all the motions of the long evening
echoing along the inner caverns
of our long years that seemed at times
so empty, filling now with the song
of my own being,
this bereft woman awakening in sorrow as if sorrow
is the genius composer of a thoroughly modern music.

Living Alone is a Kind of Weight

I read in the newspaper a rock star
thrown out of the house by his wife
climbs a light pole
and hangs himself with a bungee cord.

It's such an absurd image.
It's Dali, not Modigliani.
It's something I would have discussed with you
that night over dinner.

Living alone is a kind of weight
pushing down on you from above,
a hand on the top of your head,
fingers splayed for leverage,

shoving you down into the ground
feet first.

The Night Draws Itself Around My Throat

It's frightening
how the fictions begin to come true,
how a house creaks after

a woman tries to sell me
a burglar alarm. She is too young
to comprehend widowhood. She doesn't

need to know much about fear, her
customers bring their own,
carry it from room to room. They show her

the weakened locks, the windows exposed,
the hollow doors.
This is the night of resurrection, the oldest

terrors return. I am bolder than the child
I was, I rise up to throw light and language
like bridges across the years. Still,

my parents were home then, and now,
not even a cat, unwilling as I am
to do what it takes to endear one to me.

A New Owner

I feel my way into the autonomy of this house,
places that were yours
because territories arrange themselves
through persistence and desire. Somehow
pruning trees and hitting nails fell to you;
I of course was in charge of food and literature.
The nurturing needs of marriage are uneven,
often bulging with discord or sodden
with the inequities of mind and muscle.
Now all belongs to me at an age I can hardly reach
the high places, fearing falls, fractures,
a bloody lonely death on the cold stone floor of the garage.
So with every decision to take possession, I am the widow
as well as the mistress—freed and frightened,
older and newer. Just as there was no antidote
to your death, there is no alternative to irony.
I don't mean to say death is a cosmic joke.
That isn't at all what I mean.

Counting Weeks

I haven't counted weeks since our children
were babies; the changes in infants
can be measured daily.
It is four weeks since you died.
I grow visible in public, go
to a movie, show up where poetry is read.
Sometimes I am hugged when I tell,
sometimes there's a clumsy silence
or a low trill of sympathy.
I do not judge. Death
makes my best friends
mute but I am learning tricks
to forgive them, gratitude for what they mean
to say, feathery laughter
to brush away tension like a blackboard eraser.
No one forgets I have come alone.
Sometimes I linger. I do not forget
you are not up waiting.
I try to see myself from the outside
to determine whether I look whole yet.

Pasting Stamps on Envelopes

State flowers
grace corners
of cards I mail in gratitude.

Grim thanks,
dear friends—
I love you all

for telling me
how much you loved him,
how pure his soul,

how open his hands.
You serve
to remind me

what was lost.
I who lived
with all his flaws

and had to find
my love
in the apertures.

Ghost

I have heard of the phenomenon
where the beloved returns
from the grave as if from a tasteless joke
to resume fixing broken chair legs
and taking out the trash. I have not seen you much
these last few days, though on occasion I have
laughed or groaned at the wisp of connection
to a thread of the past. What makes trivia
so compelling? That's how a medium revealed
my mother. By the golden stains on her apron.
The long-overdue apology.
The silly nickname that will never fit anyone else.

I Lose You and Find You

When I was young and didn't know how to describe a man in a story,
I wrote of losing him, as if absence were memory made visible.

Now you are gone, you are dead. Others are rushing to fill in
this noninhabitance with descriptions I find unsettling.

You are being deconstructed down to letters and spaces like the original Torah
to be flung out among the multitudes like pieces of bread.

They seem to suggest I purposely left out those luminous parts of you
though you went on smiling just the same,

becoming a legend made out of such smiles.
It would be foolish to seek you in their scolding embellishments.

You will never be who you were because no one had the full sense of you.
It is left to me to reclaim you. I ask angels to bless my hands

while I gather your facets like shards from a broken vessel. I only record the stages.
Reconfigured, you are become the shape I apparently loved.

Edward Hopper's "Nighthawks" Makes Me Dream of Murdering A Woman

The naked horizontals of the restaurant's window keep promising dawn and revelation
but the shadows only deepen.

That night I dream the glass has disappeared; there is no longer a barrier between
my acquiescence and my need to kill. My heart agrees.

My muscles flex as my arm swings up to throw an oversize axe; you know by now
this place belongs to a woman who is still alive.

I want to take her down. I want to see her torn and peeled and bleeding. I want to throttle her
until she gives up her breath to my dead lover. But I know her.

She has a husband who beats and terrorizes her. Like Hopper's couples they will
always be stuck together. They will never touch each other again.

I'm grateful a framed window protects them. Grateful I'm constrained by daylight
in the face of its helpless width.

She Put On Your Hat

She put on your hat—
whatever made her do it?—
the twelve-year-old daughter of our domestic
asked if she could have your wool tweed hat,
the one I bought you in Ireland,
and though I wondered what she was up to
I said yes. I saw her bend down,
lift it off the pile waiting to go to the thrift shop,
plop it on top of her dark hair, give it a little
twist, place her hand on her hip
which suddenly seemed to curve
of itself, grin a shrewd grin at me
and in front of my eyes turn Peruvian,
a flirty saucy woman on her way to the market.

How did this happen, my love?

Every Day I Throw Away Something

Every day I throw away something
that belonged to you, the house
gets bigger, it inflates like the inside of a balloon,
grows hollow without you.
Where will it end, this expansion, and where will I rest
within it,
and where will I lay my shoes?

Playing With Your Shoes

Laughter was unexpected.
Our daughters, helping me
sort things out, start playing
with your shoes. Amy
finds two pair she can wear
to work. They are nearly
new, and she is so much like you.

Jessie remembers
putting on your shoes when
she was six or seven,
pretending to be you
home from work, asking
"What's new?"

After they leave,
there are still your shirts to do,
pants, belts, eyeglasses,
the change on the dresser,
the pipes—the pipes
you finally stopped smoking
when you needed breath to walk—
the stale shreds of tobacco,
unread books,
jackets and sweaters and pictures,
anomalous bikini underwear—
am I telling too much?

They are mine to touch
and sift, decide what to save,
what to give away.
Every room in the house
bears your scent.

You left me weary
work. I used to hum
when I worked, but now
I concentrate, consider
the moral consequence
of this disownment.

I Could Say It's Tobacco

I could say that rankness,
that miasmic stink, is tobacco,
I could narrow it, name it
pipe tobacco, give you
the brand, and yet
you wouldn't know the exact
smell, and I wouldn't know
how to add in his skin and its
exudate, the particular quality
of his chemical body, the clothes
he wore, the fabric, the frequency
of laundering, the soap,
the cycle, the day of the week,
the heat of the day, how measured
his breath, how wet
the air, the sum, the total
wall of smell I meet formed
of all this and you
wouldn't know it. All this
lives in my house,
in his closet, on his side
of the bed, his pillow.
Him. I am giving away
his clothing, discarding
his shoes, I must, his ties
are out of date, his belts
don't fit me. Next I'll tackle
his underwear, his odor
folded inside every drawer.
His smell is joining the air outside.

It is draining out of the rooms,
leaving through the open window,
the thin slit I could not block at the door.
It takes weeks,
the scent is getting weaker.
I keep one sweater
so I can press my face
into the thick wool of a sleeve
while I inhale deeply.

I Began With Frayed Sweaters

I began with frayed sweaters, then the stained shirts,
dated jackets—it seemed easy,
as if I had grabbed the right thread
for the quick unraveling.
The second stage,
when each garment got weighed
before it was folded and packed to be given away,
should have foretold
the final phase. What was it
about the finer fabrics, the camel hair jacket,
the tweed, the raw silk, the slim leather boots
hardly worn, that made it so hard to discard them?
Plenty and deprivation lay side by side.
He held fast to everything, wore some clothes
threadbare, saved the favorites
by scant use, leaving them less bent to his shape.
I could give up at last what most reminded me
of him, but couldn't bear to lose
the good suits he never wore. Yet they fit
no one I knew, no friend, no family member,
as if they waited only his return
and if he came back, they'd urge him
to put them on, enjoy the wanton pleasure
of their feel against his skin,
teach him what he could not learn before.

The Widow/Widowers Support Group

The newly-bereaved gather
in the enormous neighborhood synagogue
that also houses higher causes.
Unmoored, we stray the corridors
behind a leader who tries to find an empty room for us
so we may begin.
An old widower dryly muses
on how the Marx Brothers would have choreographed this scene.
I will look to him in weeks to come
to tell a joke now and then, and he will,
as we retell the facts of the weeks just past
in which we have all moved shocked
out of complacency like survivors of quakes
and car wrecks. Why do I go?
I don't share their guilts or their particularities.
I meet them here as if on some other plane,
where we have become a kinship of magicians
who incarnate, alchemists who transfigure, gods who resurrect.
Belief is not essential: As soon as the dead are named, they rise and walk among us.

How the Dead Crowd Our Closets

Once a week the bereft meet to speak aloud
the crushing departures of our dead spouses.

Between the earthquake and the abyss lies the harrowing naming of the ways
death has wrecked our houses. How do I tell them what I have never known?

Tell them you smoke marijuana
to help you sleep.

While the other widows are touting ativan,
valerian root, hot baths with lavender, my devil begins to heal with attitude.

Tell them you have a dialogue every night
with your dead husband; you get to put words in his mouth.

One woman's husband lives on in eternal urbanity on her answering machine.
One woman throws out her husband's toothbrush, quickly retrieves it.

Tell them you've thrown out nearly all of his clothes
but sometimes you wear his Jockey shorts.

We learn to be widows from history,
from old goats and lechers, from our grandmothers, from operettas and rumor.

We tell our stories: How the shrouds of the dead crowd our closets in cashmere.
Chenille and challis dangle from hangers, lint and silkworms rustle in the drawers.

Tell them: In our kitchens, when we set the table for one, we will learn to live alone.
In our beds, we will learn to be widows.

Night Mind Awake

I sleep curled and dreaming like a fetus on the brink of enlightenment
and I wake hungry for ultimate answers the way I read books as a child
but I'm left at dawn with a smoking gun and the mineral smell of a dream.

It's sometimes not that hard, and it's sometimes a kick, to fill in the rest.
All I have to do is rub and tickle the core symbols uncovered by Joseph or
Jung or Freud or the Aborigines, and I've come up with a pretty good story.

Awake at night, I'm stripped of defenses.

Awake and stricken as few cars go by and the stars come and go untended,
the shades drawn, my eyes closed, I can feel the changing light in my bones.
Thinking of you at night differs from dreaming: The past is less clear.

I remember why we married but I can't remember when I began to love you.

These Poems Have Not Been About Him

These poems I've been writing
have not been about him.

In most of them he does not come clear
in some definitive way
to tell me who is absent.

His absence consists of such light moments
I dare not share them
lest our marriage seem inconsequential
and my tears laughable.

These pieces of anguish are unpatterned
and appear suddenly.
They do not add up.
Death remains a philosophy and a religion.

In my denial I feel infinitely healthy.

If death is the instant he drew his last breath,
it seemed almost voluntary.

Now, he appeared to decide, *now I'll stop.*
It was so quiet, I wasn't certain;
so inevitable, I nearly shrugged.

Well, what did you expect,
I could have asked myself.

The Rings

When I was twisting the ring off your finger
and hit the thickness of the middle knuckle
and had to leave you alone
to get a jar of vaseline so I could ease it off
the rest of the way
you were still alive. Breathing
like a broken motor. Your eyes, open and pale,
looked, it seemed, at me.
I think I was talking to you. I hope I told you
what I was doing, and why I couldn't wait any longer.
I wrote out a dialogue
after you died. As always, you were generous.
You said you forgave me.

Months later, when I was twisting the ring off my finger,
my finger became engorged like a sausage,
it turned crimson with outrage. I thought
it would pop off. I stopped
breathing. Why this moment
and not the one before, or next week,
some poetic anniversary.
I immersed my hand in a bowl of ice and waited
for the chill shrinkage of our 43 years together,
then drenched my finger in liquid soap and twisted hard.
It hurt like hell. I kept twisting. Oh how it hurt,
and I cried out, mortally wounded
in that fleshless desert between the body and the mind.
A line was being drawn, thin as my ring.
Each time I cross over the white border
my ring once covered, I am more marked, more naked.

Where Mourning Lies

Someone said, this is what it's like:
one minute you're going along as if nothing happened,
the next minute you're prostrate with grief.
Ashamed, I realize I have not been prostrate.
I have been congested, vague, swept by trivial weeping.
I have lost a blue purse,
but haven't even approached the truly insane
waves of wailing bringing me to my knees.
I can almost make out that ancient keening
as if I have been eavesdropping all my life through walls of loss.
I have heard approximations of anguish from the throats of actors.
I once heard a tape of mother gorillas mourning their dead babies:
a choral howling soaring above forests of other animal noises.
I have missed you pore by pore without once screaming.
I have heard you walk into my house and vanish.
I have reached for your hand and whimpered.
Where in me is the cry of my inconsolable heart?

The Garden You Tended

Everything that's died in the garden you tended
has started falling, piling up, drying out, debris of lives that have ended.

I don't know whether the gist of the mystery hides in what lives
or in what dies or whether both must be aligned before they can be blended

with the permanent air, your influence extended
like the newly-budded Mandarin tangerine tree which stayed alive

in spite of my almost wanton abandonment. When I saw that it lived
beyond you and mocked me with its vigor, I pretended

it was fatally flawed in the pot. My neglect was easily defended.
As I withheld light and water, its parched fruit dropped. Not one lived.

Brittle stems, yellow leaves were what bitterness engendered.
My heart began to break further. I surrendered,

gave it sustenance, dragged it closer to the sun. Soon leaves opened,
my ambivalence seemingly mended. It lived

on a few more months, nearly a year.
The tree is dead. I'd better feed what lives.

The Snapshots I Never Framed

It's not the pictures I made bigger, matted, framed, hung
until they became iconic, it's the rest of the pack,
the old snaps I probably should have thrown out
in which he looked sideways, failed to smile.
I come across them. What I miss most
is the ordinary self of him, his face less perfect,
the glance least posed,
when no one was watching.
This is the face that is suddenly so real
I must force myself to remember his death.

The Life of the Word

On the side of the bed where you slept
books are piling up. When I can't sleep, I reach out and grab
whatever comes to hand, old newspapers, articles I saved unread
from so many sad sick Sundays.
It's no use, words are still seeping into each other. I keep
a lined pad, pens, just in case. Last night I picked one up
as one picks up a foreign object on a familiar street
and miraculously the word returned,
the body of the work woke to the surge of idea in the middle of the night.
There was no need to sneak out for fear of disturbing you,
no need to suppress the urge to pound you awake.
In this writing outside of dream and drugs and mourning,
God assures me there is enough blood on my hands, it is time to confess.
It is time to say I need, I want, I will never forget you. I will reinvent you
the way I remember my parents and the childhood years of our children
and the betrayals of friends. I will dive down
into lies so deep the truth of what I mean to say will return in time to forgive me.

After the Dream of the Faceless Man's Body

After the dream of the faceless man's body
pressed so hard against mine there was no room
for air or any movement except yearning,
I began to be better at locating documents
requested of me by my accountant.
When I spoke on the phone,
I was no longer vacillating.
I was able to get the leaking toilet repaired.
There is much more to be done.
And there is the possibility of happiness.

I Never Got To Know My Mother

Though she lived longer,
I never got to know my mother
the way I got to know you.
Your eyes,
white and milky near the end,
grew light with the knowledge of us
and how I shall go on by myself.
And so it is I believe you approve
of the way I organize my day,
letting the tears fall unstructured
and unplanned, letting the work
arrange itself around the mourning
instead of the other way around.
And if it happens I sometimes need your approval
now, when I did not always wait for your living
hands to bless my whims and indiscretions
it is because we are more one than we were
in life, less at odds, less at cross-purposes.

Unnatural Habits

I am growing too fond of living alone.
My innate coarseness is spreading over this house.
On his side of the kitchen table
I pile mail to be read at leisure, of which I have none
because leisure seems sinful in a climate of mourning.
The dishes get washed then drain upside down for days.
I become drawn to death by elegies of unhealthy eating,
tempted toward burial in clothes I no longer love.
One half of me has already dissolved.
The remainder gives thanks for Christmas catalogues.
I could become a cow-girl or a Victoria Secret slut.
I could buy a Neiman-Marcus fourteen-carat-gold cover-up thing for $27,000.
My damaged body is moving out into the world without me,
trying on poses and colors while I watch from a distance,
naked except for what I found in my closet the day after he died.
I tried on everything but nothing fit, as if I had grown extra limbs.
I was not in my garments. I had left myself.
Now I go to the malls, upscale and downscale stores full of costumes.
Seductive fabrics, styles so young I could become available.
Get my heart broken all over again.

The Places We Went Together

I often went to see foreign films with him.
I went to the Los Angeles County Art Museum with him.
We went to Ireland together.
We went to his home town in Hungary.
I went to Amsterdam with him.
We travelled to Florence three different times.
We went to Toronto together, and then Montreal, and Niagara Falls twice.
I went to Alaska with him.
Once we went to Vienna.
Twice we went to Israel.
For years I went to the Mark Taper Forum with him.
I went to New York with him several times, though he said he didn't like it.
We went to London, York, Bath, the Lake district.
We visited the zoos in Los Angeles, San Diego and Santa Barbara.
I went to Mexico City with him.
We went to Bangkok and Hong Kong.
We went to Canton, Cancun, Cabo San Lucas, Costa Rica, Puerto Rico, Cuernavaca, Kuala Lumpur, Kauai and Columbus, Ohio, where his Uncle Max and Aunt Ida lived and died.
We went to Washington, D.C., Seattle, San Francisco and Indianapolis.
We went to Havana on a cruise ship.
We went to Paris together, and Madrid, and Trieste, and Venice.
We went to Boston.
We went to Naples.
We decided we would never go to Germany.

The Conference at Asilomar, at the End of the Year 1998

I did not come here to forget you.
I did not fly over mountains to these sere and distant dunes
to purge myself of mourning. How could I
when every tree I walk around is twisted into grotesque beauty
by brutal winds, and every gnarled root still holding on
reminds me how you stood your ground.

Even had you lived, I would have come alone
to sit among the seasoned meditators, digging down
on aching knees for wisdom and epiphanies,
settling for stillness and relaxed shoulders. I would have come back
feeling blissed and blessed, to fill your ears with stories.

Instead I brought you along so you could hear
the loud drumming ocean beating scalding sorrow out of me.
So you could hear me—
bowed and raw as uncut wheat in front of these simplicities: rocks,
water, sound, sand—crying much more than in my half-empty bed.

That is what I came here to do:
To purify with waves of salt water the stinging assaults of memory.
And like you, to move on.

The Crack About to Open Up (February 28, 1999)

I had been noting the anniversary of Ted's death on the 29th
day of each month. February, 1999 was not a leap year.

In the crack about to open up between 11:59 tonight and 12:01 tomorrow,
in the abyss of that missing 29th day when I would have said
   now it is nine months since he died

I may find myself elsewhere, in the kitchen washing dirt off the strawberries,
on the internet checking my mail; I could forget to note a split in time,
   a phantom anniversary severed from its mnemonic function.

On the day he died, we conceived a prolonged silence together.
Because death plants for eternity the seed of silence, nine months is not a turning
   and it is no sin to watch television or read a newspaper.

And yet I think of him tonight, turning over in my mind the quick time that's gone
from mindless grief to mundane life.
   My mourning is still young.

If They Found Your Bones

If they found your bones, stripped,
salt gray, slick like peeled bark,
a thousand years from now
what would they know of you?
Did the sewing needles you held
as if they completed your breath
ever nick a single phalanx
in your zeal and probe
for perfection, never in yourself,
but in each stitch of holy purpose
that flowed like shy miracles from
the tips of your dextrous fingers
to the form and trim of fabric?
Did the wear on your soles and toes
show you ran like wildebeests as a boy
(outran antisemitic thugs, you told me)?
Did your kneecaps wear out where you
knelt as a man to pin a hem
accurately? Big fingers:
can they tell that? Thank God
for your big fingers. The tongue
has no bones: maybe not
something they'd care about anyway.
Your skull nearly naked when we met,
I neglected to read its subtleties,
only marvelled at the long span
of your forehead. Glasses, tweeds,
pipes, you resembled an academic,
but only asked to be

some ordinary working stiff
since you learned in the camps
to become a face
blended safely into the crowd.
No man stood out in his rags
and bruises unless
he made a wrong move
and drew fire. You learned
to keep your eyes downcast.
A thousand years from now,
some zealous archeologist
would have to take the time
to sort your bones from the rest
to know the difference.

You Are Dead

Last night I dreamt I kissed another man.
Full on the mouth. My tongue deep
inside his mouth. We lay together, my back
against his chest, and he held me curled
and defended as if his arms were wings.
I know this reads like the start of a cheap novel in almost any context,
even the accidental betrayals of sleep.
But I swear this is not a dream about fucking and forgetting.
It is a dream about a man who yearns to be touched again
lying still in the skin of a woman who wants desperately to touch him.
Touch is what my body remembers. You are dead.
This is a dream about what you burned into me.

The First Yahrzeit

I

Each ending was once a beginning: a first-
born child, a sliver of moon, a commemoration.

II

In the midst of mourning, I became more Jewish.
I sought instruction from ancestors
who worked death into their daily lives,
praying with their hands and feet. They believed
devoutly in the moon's arc and the balm of time,
and they said so, and they wrote it down:
one week for the shock of grief,
one moon's turning for deep breathing,
ten more cycles for a kind of acclimation,
then a candle at the end of a year, a year later
another, if need be forever,
until our pain consoles us.

III

Tonight I light the first Yahrzeit candle.

IV

At sundown
in the sanctuary of my kitchen
with its sapphire tiles
and its white reflective walls,
I will ignite the candle and become
memory's unwilling host.

V

On my Christian calendar, Gauguin's pagan paintings on every page,
I counted ten more days to the anniversary of your death
but a post card from the mortuary reminded me
I am a Jew stretched between the lunar and the linear.
It is the moon that rules the Hebrew year, month by month purging blood,
pulling to itself the earth's tides, dictating to the faithful its adamant cycles.
I will light the Yahrzeit candle tonight
but how will I live the next ten days?   Must I cry
on every one of them?

VI

In the beginning,
when the match is struck
and laid to the wick
and the wick crackles
as the flame catches, flickers
and swoons, out of breath,
then flares into an ecstatic leap toward heaven
seething into the night
into its allotted duration,
into its memorial season,
into the death year ending,
there is comfort.

VII

The flame is my guardian, I shall not fear.
It illuminates the corners of my kitchen.
It gilds the windows.
When I am giddy with despair
a ribbon of fire unravels off the ceiling
to lead me out of the labyrinth of darkness.
If I wake in the night it is there.
If I sleep through the night it is there.
It is a beacon into morning,
merging with dawn the way stars will.

VIII

I keep count
to the last
of the ten days marked
on my calendar,
the Gregorian day on which you died
one year ago.

IX

The next day, which falls on the date
which might have become our 44th anniversary
I hover above your grave, which is shrouded
until an ancient ritual of confluence and revelation
tells me it is time
to uncover the new bronze plaque
in the intimate presence of community.
Our children who spoke in whispers near your deathbed
and in beauty at your funeral
are wordless here.
Family and friends
take up the praise and anecdote,
and at the end
we pray.
I bend, pull the plastic cover off, unveil
your name. Date of birth. Date of death.

X

The next day nothing has changed.
Maybe ten more days must pass,
ten years. The rest of my life
before I know what is over.